Buttermilk Fried Chicken

Irresistible Recipes and Tips for Perfectly Crispy and Flavorful Fried Chicken

BUTTERMILK FRIED CHICKEN

First edition. December 8, 2023.

ISBN: 979-8223226765

Written by john ahmad.

Table of Contents

John Ahmad

Introduction

Welcome to the world of irresistibly crispy and flavorful buttermilk fried chicken! In this cookbook, we will embark on a culinary journey exploring the art of preparing this beloved dish. Whether you're a seasoned cook or a novice in the kitchen, this book will guide you through step-by-step instructions and expert tips to ensure your fried chicken turns out perfect every time.

Buttermilk fried chicken is more than just a meal; it's a cultural icon and a symbol of comfort and indulgence. The magic lies in the buttermilk brine, a technique that tenderizes the chicken while infusing it with a delightful tangy flavor. We'll delve into the science behind buttermilk brining, understanding how it enhances the texture and taste of our chicken.

In this cookbook, you'll find a diverse collection of recipes ranging from the classic and timeless to the innovative and unexpected. We'll explore traditional Southern-style chicken, bold and spicy variations, healthier alternatives, and even sweet desserts featuring fried chicken.

Beyond the recipes, we'll also explore the world of complementary sides, sauces, and beverages that perfectly accompany our crispy creations. Whether you prefer to fry in a traditional skillet, opt for oven-baking, or explore air frying, we have you covered with helpful tips and techniques for each method.

So, tie up your apron, sharpen your culinary skills, and get ready to take your fried chicken game to the next level. Whether you're cooking for family gatherings, casual weeknight dinners, or special occasions, the recipes in this cookbook are sure to delight your taste buds and impress your guests.

Join us as we dive into the delicious world of "Buttermilk Fried Chicken." Let's get cooking

Chapter 1: The Art of Buttermilk Brining

Brining is the secret to achieving exceptionally tender and flavorful fried chicken, and buttermilk brining takes it to a whole new level. In this chapter, we'll explore the ins and outs of this essential technique, understanding why it's a game-changer for your fried chicken.

1.1 The Science of Buttermilk Brining

Brining is a culinary process that involves soaking meat in a saltwater solution to enhance its moisture and flavor. Buttermilk brining takes this concept to another level by adding tangy buttermilk to the mix. But why does buttermilk work so well in this process?

When chicken is soaked in buttermilk, the natural lactic acid present in the buttermilk helps break down the muscle fibers, resulting in a more tender and succulent meat. Additionally, the acidity of buttermilk acts as a flavor conduit, infusing the chicken with a subtle tang that perfectly balances the richness of the fried coating.

1.2 Benefits of Buttermilk Brining

The benefits of buttermilk brining are numerous, making it a must-try technique for any fried chicken enthusiast.

Firstly, buttermilk brining ensures the chicken stays moist and juicy during frying. As the chicken absorbs the brine, it retains more moisture, preventing it from drying out during the frying process.

Secondly, the buttermilk's acidity adds a pleasant tangy flavor to the chicken, elevating the taste to a whole new level. This delightful contrast of flavors keeps your taste buds engaged with each crispy bite.

Furthermore, buttermilk brining enhances the chicken's tenderness, making the meat easily fall off the bone. It also creates a perfect canvas for the seasoning, allowing the flavors to penetrate deep into the meat.

1.3 Brining Time and Temperature

To achieve the best results with buttermilk brining, it's essential to consider the brining time and temperature.

The brining time can vary depending on the size and thickness of the chicken cuts. Generally, smaller cuts like chicken tenders may require a shorter brining time, while larger cuts like whole chicken pieces may need more time to fully absorb the brine. As a rule of thumb, brining times can range from 30 minutes to overnight in the refrigerator.

Regarding temperature, it's crucial to keep the chicken refrigerated during the brining process to prevent bacteria growth. The ideal refrigerator temperature for brining is below 40°F (4°C). If you choose to brine at room temperature, do so for a shorter duration and keep a close eye on the chicken to ensure it remains safe to eat.

1.4 Choosing the Right Chicken Cuts

The choice of chicken cuts plays a significant role in the success of your buttermilk brined fried chicken.

Bone-in, skin-on chicken pieces tend to be the most popular choice for fried chicken, as they offer the best balance of flavor and texture. Chicken thighs, drumsticks, and wings are great options for their juiciness and ability to hold up well during frying.

If you prefer leaner cuts, boneless, skinless chicken breasts or tenders can also be used. However, these leaner cuts may require slightly shorter brining times to avoid over-tenderization.

Ultimately, the choice of chicken cuts depends on personal preference, but each cut can be made deliciously tender and flavorful through the magic of buttermilk brining.

With a solid understanding of the science, benefits, and techniques of buttermilk brining, you're now equipped to elevate your fried chicken game to new heights. In the next chapter, we'll dive into the exciting world of "Classic Buttermilk Fried Chicken," where we'll master the art of creating a timeless and unforgettable fried chicken recipe.

Chapter 2: Classic Buttermilk Fried Chicken

In this chapter, we'll delve into the iconic and timeless recipe of classic buttermilk fried chicken. Get ready to master the art of creating a mouthwatering dish that's guaranteed to please everyone at the table.

2.1 The Classic Buttermilk Brined Chicken

Ingredients:

- 1 whole chicken or chicken pieces (thighs, drumsticks, and/or wings)
- 2 cups buttermilk
- 2 tablespoons salt
- 1 teaspoon black pepper
- 1 teaspoon paprika
- 1/2 teaspoon garlic powder
- 1/2 teaspoon onion powder

Instructions:

1. In a large mixing bowl, combine buttermilk, salt, black pepper, paprika, garlic powder, and onion powder. Stir until the salt dissolves and the spices are well incorporated.
2. Add the chicken pieces to the buttermilk mixture, ensuring they are completely submerged. Cover the bowl with plastic wrap and refrigerate for at least 4 hours or preferably overnight. This allows the buttermilk brine to work its magic, tenderizing the chicken and infusing it with flavor.

2.2 The Perfect Blend of Spices

Ingredients:

- 1 cup all-purpose flour

- 1 teaspoon salt
- 1/2 teaspoon black pepper
- 1/2 teaspoon paprika
- 1/2 teaspoon garlic powder
- 1/2 teaspoon onion powder
- 1/4 teaspoon cayenne pepper (adjust to taste for spiciness)

Instructions:

In a shallow dish or pie plate, combine the all-purpose flour, salt, black pepper, paprika, garlic powder, onion powder, and cayenne pepper. Mix well to create the perfect blend of spices for coating the chicken.

2.3 Achieving a Crispy Golden Crust

Ingredients:

- Vegetable oil or peanut oil, for frying

Instructions:

1. In a heavy-bottomed skillet or Dutch oven, add enough oil to come about 2 inches up the sides of the pan. Heat the oil over medium-high heat until it reaches 350°F (175°C). A deep-frying thermometer will help you monitor the temperature accurately.
2. While the oil is heating, remove the chicken pieces from the buttermilk brine, allowing any excess buttermilk to drip off. Dredge the chicken in the seasoned flour mixture, ensuring each piece is evenly coated.
3. Gently place the coated chicken pieces in the hot oil, being careful not to overcrowd the pan. Fry the chicken in batches if necessary.
4. Fry the chicken for about 12-15 minutes, turning occasionally, until it's cooked through and reaches an internal temperature of 165°F (74°C). The chicken should be golden brown and crispy on the outside.
5. Once the chicken is done, use a slotted spoon or tongs to remove it from the oil, allowing any excess oil to drain.

2.4 Serving Suggestions and Classic Sides

1. Serve your classic buttermilk fried chicken with these delicious sides:
2. Buttermilk Biscuits: Flaky and tender, these biscuits are the perfect accompaniment to fried chicken. Spread with butter and honey for a delightful treat.
3. Mashed Potatoes and Gravy: Creamy mashed potatoes smothered in rich gravy create the ultimate comfort food combination.
4. Southern-Style Coleslaw: A refreshing and tangy coleslaw balances the richness of the fried chicken and adds a crunchy texture to the meal.
5. Cornbread: A classic Southern side dish, cornbread adds a touch of sweetness to complement the savory flavors of the fried chicken.

2.5 Variations on the Classic Recipe

1. Explore these creative variations on the classic recipe:
2. Spicy Buttermilk Fried Chicken: Add extra cayenne pepper or chili powder to the flour mixture for a fiery kick.
3. Herb-Roasted Buttermilk Fried Chicken: Incorporate chopped fresh herbs, such as rosemary, thyme, or sage, into the flour mixture for an aromatic twist.
4. Lemon-Pepper Buttermilk Fried Chicken: Grate lemon zest and add ground black pepper to the flour mixture for a zesty flavor boost.
5. Buttermilk Fried Chicken Tenders: Use boneless chicken tenders for a quick and convenient alternative that's perfect for appetizers or kids' meals.

2.6 Leftover Magic: Reinventing Fried Chicken

Don't let any leftover fried chicken go to waste! Try these creative ideas for repurposing your classic buttermilk fried chicken:

Chicken and Waffles: Serve the leftover fried chicken atop fluffy waffles and drizzle with maple syrup for a delightful sweet and savory combination.

Fried Chicken Sandwich: Create a crispy chicken sandwich with your favorite toppings, such as lettuce, tomato, pickles, and a tangy sauce.

Chicken Salad: Chop up the leftover fried chicken and toss it with fresh greens, avocado, cherry tomatoes, and your favorite dressing for a hearty salad.

Fried Chicken Tacos: Fill soft tortillas with sliced fried chicken, shredded lettuce, diced tomatoes, and a zesty avocado crema for a taco night twist.

With the classic buttermilk fried chicken recipe mastered, you'll have a go-to dish that never disappoints. Get ready to impress your loved ones with this timeless favorite that brings comfort and joy to every meal. In the next chapter, we'll turn up the heat and explore the world of "Spicy Buttermilk Fried Chicken," where we'll add some thrilling flavor variations to our fried chicken repertoire.

Chapter 3: Spicy Buttermilk Fried Chicken

In this chapter, we'll take the classic buttermilk fried chicken to a whole new level by adding a fiery kick with spicy seasonings. Get ready to tantalize your taste buds with a mouthwatering blend of heat and flavor, balanced to perfection.

3.1 Adding a Fiery Kick with Spicy Seasonings
Ingredients:

- 1 teaspoon cayenne pepper
- 1 teaspoon smoked paprika
- 1/2 teaspoon ground cumin
- 1/2 teaspoon chili powder
- 1/4 teaspoon cayenne pepper (for extra heat, adjust to taste)
- 1/4 teaspoon garlic powder
- 1/4 teaspoon onion powder
- 1/4 teaspoon salt

Instructions:

1. To create our spicy seasoning blend, combine cayenne pepper, smoked paprika, ground cumin, chili powder, additional cayenne pepper (if desired), garlic powder, onion powder, and salt in a shallow dish. Mix well to ensure the spices are evenly distributed.
2. Prepare the buttermilk brined chicken pieces as outlined in Chapter 2.2. Once the chicken is ready, generously coat each piece in the spicy seasoning mixture, pressing the spices onto the chicken to adhere well.
3. Continue with the frying instructions from Chapter 2.3 to achieve a crispy golden crust that encapsulates the

mouthwatering spiciness.

3.2 Balancing Heat and Flavor for the Perfect Spice Level

When working with spicy seasonings, finding the perfect balance between heat and flavor is essential. To achieve the ideal spice level for your taste preferences, consider the following tips:

Taste as you season: Add the spicy seasoning mixture to the chicken gradually, tasting as you go. This allows you to control the heat and adjust it according to your liking.

Pair with complementary flavors: Incorporate ingredients that balance the heat, such as sweet honey, tangy citrus, or cooling yogurt-based sauces. This contrast in flavors creates a well-rounded and enjoyable eating experience.

Cater to individual preferences: If you're serving a group, consider offering different levels of spiciness, such as mild, medium, and hot, by adjusting the amount of cayenne pepper in the seasoning blend.

3.3 Cooling Accompaniments to Complement the Heat

To complement the fiery kick of our spicy buttermilk fried chicken, serve it with refreshing accompaniments that help cool down the palate:

Buttermilk Ranch Dressing: A classic choice, buttermilk ranch dressing provides a creamy and cooling contrast to the heat of the fried chicken.

Pickles: Crisp and tangy pickles offer a delightful bite that refreshes the taste buds between spicy chicken bites.

Coleslaw with a Twist: Prepare a creamy coleslaw with shredded cabbage, carrots, and a hint of sweetness from diced apples or raisins. This not only cools down the heat but also adds an extra layer of flavor.

Cucumber Yogurt Sauce: Create a simple cucumber yogurt sauce with grated cucumber, Greek yogurt, dill, garlic, and lemon juice. The cool and creamy sauce complements the spice and adds a refreshing touch.

With the spicy buttermilk fried chicken recipe mastered, you'll have a knockout dish that's sure to impress anyone who loves a little heat.

So get ready to turn up the temperature and enjoy the fiery goodness of this spicy creation. Next up, we'll explore the world of "Buttermilk Fried Chicken Tenders," a versatile and fun variation that's perfect for snacking, appetizers, or kids' meals.

Chapter 4: Buttermilk Fried Chicken Tenders

In this chapter, we'll explore the delightful world of buttermilk fried chicken tenders – a versatile and fun variation perfect for snacks, appetizers, or kids' meals. Get ready to indulge in crispy and tender chicken tenders that are sure to become a family favorite.

4.1 The Irresistible Buttermilk Fried Chicken Tenders
Ingredients:

- 1 pound chicken tenders
- 2 cups buttermilk
- 1 teaspoon salt
- 1/2 teaspoon black pepper
- 1/2 teaspoon paprika
- 1/4 teaspoon garlic powder
- 1/4 teaspoon onion powder

Instructions:

1. In a bowl, whisk together buttermilk, salt, black pepper, paprika, garlic powder, and onion powder to create the buttermilk brine.
2. Place the chicken tenders in the buttermilk brine, ensuring they are fully submerged. Cover the bowl with plastic wrap and refrigerate for at least 1 hour, allowing the tenders to absorb the flavors and become tender.

4.2 Creating Different Dipping Sauces

A variety of dipping sauces takes buttermilk fried chicken tenders to the next level. Here are some delicious options to consider:

Honey Mustard Sauce: Mix together equal parts of honey and Dijon mustard, with a pinch of salt and black pepper. This sweet and tangy sauce pairs perfectly with the crispy tenders.

Barbecue Sauce: For a smoky and tangy kick, serve the tenders with your favorite store-bought or homemade barbecue sauce.

Ranch Dressing: A classic choice, ranch dressing adds creamy and herby goodness to the chicken tenders.

Spicy Sriracha Mayo: Combine mayonnaise with Sriracha sauce for a creamy and spicy dip that complements the tenders' crunchy texture.

Sweet Chili Sauce: Serve the tenders with a sweet and slightly spicy chili sauce for a burst of flavor.

Feel free to mix and match these sauces or get creative with your own unique concoctions.

4.3 Fun and Creative Serving Ideas

Elevate the presentation of your buttermilk fried chicken tenders with these fun and creative serving ideas:

Bento Box Delight: Pack the chicken tenders in a bento box alongside a selection of dipping sauces, sliced veggies, and fruit for a cute and convenient meal.

Slider Party: Turn the tenders into mini sliders by placing them in soft slider buns with lettuce, tomato slices, and your favorite sauce.

Skewer Sensation: Thread the chicken tenders onto bamboo skewers for a fun and portable party appetizer. Serve them with dipping sauces on the side.

Kids' Favorite: Serve the tenders with smiley-faced fries or other kid-friendly sides for a meal that will win over even the pickiest eaters.

Tenders and Tots: Pair the tenders with crispy tater tots and offer a variety of dipping sauces for a nostalgic and satisfying combo.

With the endless possibilities of buttermilk fried chicken tenders, you'll have a go-to dish that's perfect for any occasion. From family dinners to game-day snacks and everything in between, these tender and crispy chicken tenders will be a hit. In the next chapter, we'll explore the world of "Buttermilk Fried Chicken Sandwiches," where we'll take our fried chicken between buns for a scrumptious and satisfying treat.

Chapter 5: Buttermilk Fried Chicken Sandwiches

In this chapter, we'll elevate our buttermilk fried chicken to new heights by sandwiching it between buns, creating a delicious and satisfying treat. Get ready to savor the crispy and flavorful fried chicken combined with a medley of mouthwatering toppings and spreads.

5.1 Elevating Your Fried Chicken Between Buns

Ingredients:

- Buttermilk fried chicken pieces (from Chapter 2)
- Soft hamburger buns or brioche buns

Instructions:

1. Prepare the buttermilk fried chicken as per the classic recipe outlined in Chapter 2, ensuring it's perfectly crispy and golden.
2. Select your favorite soft hamburger buns or brioche buns to hold the flavorful fried chicken.

5.2 Building a Delicious and Satisfying Sandwich

Now comes the fun part – building a mouthwatering buttermilk fried chicken sandwich! Consider these delightful elements:

Crunchy Coleslaw: Top the fried chicken with a generous portion of tangy and crunchy coleslaw, providing a refreshing contrast to the crispy chicken.

Pickles: Add a layer of dill pickles or bread-and-butter pickles for a delightful zing that balances the richness of the fried chicken.

Lettuce and Tomato: Fresh lettuce leaves and ripe tomato slices bring a burst of color and freshness to the sandwich.

Cheese: For an extra indulgent touch, melt a slice of your favorite cheese over the hot fried chicken. Cheddar, Swiss, or pepper jack are great options.

Special Sauce: Create a signature sauce by mixing mayonnaise with your favorite hot sauce, honey, and a squeeze of lemon. This homemade spicy mayo adds a unique kick to the sandwich.

Crispy Bacon: For a heavenly flavor combination, add a few strips of crispy bacon to the sandwich.

Fried Egg (optional): Take the sandwich to the next level by topping it with a fried egg, creating a decadent and satisfying meal.

Assemble your buttermilk fried chicken sandwich by layering the components to your liking, ensuring each bite is a harmonious explosion of flavors and textures.

5.3 Homemade Spreads and Condiments

Complement your buttermilk fried chicken sandwich with these homemade spreads and condiments:

Honey Butter Spread: Mix softened butter with honey for a sweet and luscious spread that pairs wonderfully with the savory fried chicken.

Chipotle Mayo: Combine mayonnaise with chipotle peppers in adobo sauce for a smoky and spicy mayo that takes the sandwich to the next level.

Avocado Aioli: Mash ripe avocados and blend them with garlic, lemon juice, and mayonnaise to create a creamy and flavorful aioli.

Jalapeño Ranch Dressing: Add minced jalapeño peppers to ranch dressing for a zesty and slightly spicy sauce.

With the creative possibilities of buttermilk fried chicken sandwiches, you'll have a scrumptious and satisfying meal that's perfect for lunch, dinner, or a weekend indulgence. The combination of crispy fried chicken, delectable toppings, and homemade spreads ensures a culinary experience that will leave you craving more. In the next chapter, we'll explore the world of "Oven-Baked Buttermilk Fried Chicken," where we'll discover a healthier twist on the classic recipe without compromising on taste.

Chapter 6: Oven-Baked Buttermilk Fried Chicken

In this chapter, we'll explore a healthier twist on the classic fried chicken – oven-baked buttermilk fried chicken. Get ready to enjoy the same crispy and flavorful chicken without the need for deep-frying, making it a guilt-free and delicious alternative.

6.1 A Healthier Twist on the Classic Fried Chicken

Ingredients:

- Buttermilk fried chicken pieces (from Chapter 2)

Instructions:

1. Start by preparing the buttermilk fried chicken as outlined in Chapter 2, ensuring the chicken is well-brined and seasoned.
2. Preheat your oven to 400°F (200°C) and place a wire rack on top of a baking sheet. The wire rack allows hot air to circulate around the chicken, promoting even browning and crispiness.
3. Remove the chicken pieces from the buttermilk brine and allow any excess buttermilk to drip off. Dredge the chicken in the seasoned flour mixture as previously described.
4. Place the coated chicken pieces on the wire rack, leaving some space between each piece to ensure they cook evenly.
5. Bake the chicken in the preheated oven for 25-30 minutes or until the internal temperature reaches 165°F (74°C). The chicken should be golden brown and crispy.

6.2 Tips for Achieving a Crispy Texture Without Deep-Frying

1. Achieving a crispy texture without deep-frying requires a few tricks. Here are some tips to ensure your oven-baked buttermilk fried chicken is as crispy as the traditional version:

2. Use a Wire Rack: Elevating the chicken pieces on a wire rack allows hot air to circulate around the chicken, preventing it from becoming soggy.

3. Lightly Coat with Oil: Before baking, lightly brush or spray the chicken pieces with vegetable oil. This helps promote browning and crispiness.

4. High Heat: Bake the chicken at a higher temperature (around 400°F/200°C) to encourage browning and crispy skin.

5. Don't Overcrowd the Pan: Give the chicken pieces enough space on the wire rack to avoid steaming and ensure proper browning.

6.3 Oven-Baked vs. Traditional Fried: Taste Comparison

Now comes the delicious moment of truth – a taste comparison between oven-baked buttermilk fried chicken and traditional deep-fried chicken.

Flavor: While the traditional fried chicken undeniably boasts a rich and deep flavor, the oven-baked version surprises with a delightful balance of flavors from the buttermilk brine and spices.

Texture: Traditional fried chicken has an unmistakably crispy and crunchy texture, but oven-baked buttermilk fried chicken holds its own with a crispy exterior and tender, juicy interior.

Health Benefits: The oven-baked version significantly reduces the amount of oil used in the cooking process, making it a healthier choice without sacrificing taste and texture.

Convenience: Oven-baked buttermilk fried chicken requires less hands-on attention and eliminates the need for handling hot oil, making it a safer and more convenient option.

In the end, the taste comparison may vary depending on personal preference, but oven-baked buttermilk fried chicken proves to be a worthy contender for those seeking a healthier alternative without compromising on flavor and texture.

With the oven-baked buttermilk fried chicken recipe mastered, you'll have a guilt-free option that satisfies your cravings for deliciously crispy chicken. Next up, we'll explore the world of "Buttermilk Fried Chicken Wings," a finger-licking variation that's perfect for parties and game-day gatherings.

Chapter 7: Buttermilk Fried Chicken Wings

In this chapter, get ready to indulge in finger-licking recipes for buttermilk fried chicken wings. We'll explore various flavor profiles to suit every taste, and we'll share party platter ideas and an array of delectable sauces to accompany these crowd-pleasing wings.

7.1 Finger-Licking Recipes for Chicken Wings
Ingredients:

- Chicken wings (party wings or drumettes)
- 2 cups buttermilk
- 1 teaspoon salt
- 1/2 teaspoon black pepper
- 1/2 teaspoon paprika
- 1/2 teaspoon garlic powder
- 1/2 teaspoon onion powder

Instructions:

1. In a bowl, whisk together buttermilk, salt, black pepper, paprika, garlic powder, and onion powder to create the buttermilk brine.
2. Place the chicken wings in the buttermilk brine, ensuring they are fully submerged. Cover the bowl with plastic wrap and refrigerate for at least 1 hour, allowing the wings to marinate and become tender.

7.2 Exploring Various Flavor Profiles

Now it's time to explore a variety of flavor profiles to elevate your buttermilk fried chicken wings:

Classic Buffalo Wings: Toss the fried wings in a classic buffalo sauce made from melted butter and hot sauce, and serve with celery sticks and blue cheese or ranch dressing.

Honey BBQ Wings: Coat the wings in a sweet and smoky barbecue sauce infused with honey for a finger-licking treat.

Teriyaki Wings: Glaze the wings with a delicious teriyaki sauce, garnish with sesame seeds and green onions, and serve over steamed rice for an Asian-inspired twist.

Garlic Parmesan Wings: Toss the wings in a mixture of melted butter, minced garlic, and grated Parmesan cheese for a flavorful and indulgent option.

Lemon Pepper Wings: Sprinkle the fried wings with a zesty blend of lemon zest, black pepper, and salt for a refreshing and tangy experience.

Sweet Chili Lime Wings: Combine sweet chili sauce with lime juice and a hint of soy sauce to create a sweet and tangy coating for the wings.

Spicy Korean Wings: Toss the wings in a spicy gochujang sauce, and serve with a side of pickled vegetables for a bold and unique flavor.

7.3 Party Platter Ideas and Sauces

Create an enticing party platter by serving an assortment of buttermilk fried chicken wings with an array of delicious sauces:

Wing Sampler Platter: Arrange an assortment of wings with different flavors on a large platter, creating a tempting and colorful display.

Dipping Sauce Bar: Set up a station with various dipping sauces, such as ranch, blue cheese, honey mustard, and BBQ, so guests can customize their wing dipping experience.

Slider-Style Wings: Serve the wings in slider buns with lettuce and tomato for a fun and convenient party snack.

Wing Skewers: Thread the wings onto bamboo skewers for easy-to-eat finger food that guests can enjoy without getting their hands messy.

With the diverse flavor profiles and party platter ideas, your buttermilk fried chicken wings will be the star of any gathering. Whether it's a game-day party or a casual get-together, these finger-licking wings will keep everyone coming back for more. In the next chapter, we'll explore the world of "Sweet Buttermilk Fried Chicken Desserts," where we'll unveil surprising and delightful sweet treats featuring fried chicken.

Chapter 8: Buttermilk Ranch Dressing

In this chapter, we'll delve into the world of buttermilk ranch dressing – the perfect accompaniment for fried chicken. We'll explore the differences between homemade and store-bought ranch dressing in a taste-off, and we'll discover creative uses for any leftover ranch dressing you might have.

8.1 The Perfect Accompaniment for Fried Chicken

Ingredients:

- 1 cup mayonnaise
- 1/2 cup buttermilk
- 2 tablespoons sour cream
- 1 tablespoon chopped fresh parsley
- 1 tablespoon chopped fresh chives
- 1 teaspoon dried dill weed
- 1/2 teaspoon garlic powder
- 1/2 teaspoon onion powder
- Salt and black pepper to taste

Instructions:

1. In a bowl, whisk together mayonnaise, buttermilk, sour cream, chopped parsley, chopped chives, dried dill weed, garlic powder, and onion powder until well combined.
2. Season with salt and black pepper to taste. Adjust the consistency by adding more buttermilk for a thinner dressing or more sour cream for a thicker dressing.
3. Cover the bowl with plastic wrap and refrigerate for at least 30 minutes to allow the flavors to meld together.

8.2 Homemade Ranch vs. Store-Bought: A Taste-Off

Now it's time for a taste-off between homemade and store-bought ranch dressing:

Homemade Ranch Dressing:

The homemade version boasts a fresher and more vibrant flavor, thanks to the use of fresh herbs and spices.

You have complete control over the ingredients, allowing you to adjust the seasoning and thickness to your preference.

Homemade ranch dressing often has a creamier texture due to the use of sour cream.

Store-Bought Ranch Dressing:

Store-bought ranch dressing is convenient and readily available.

It offers a consistent flavor profile, making it a reliable option.

Some store-bought versions may contain additional preservatives and additives.

Ultimately, the choice between homemade and store-bought ranch dressing depends on your preference for a personalized and fresher taste versus convenience and consistency.

8.3 Creative Uses for Leftover Ranch Dressing

Don't let any leftover ranch dressing go to waste! Get creative with these delicious uses:

Dip It: Aside from being a classic dip for fried chicken, ranch dressing pairs well with an array of vegetables, potato chips, and even pizza crust.

Salad Dressing: Thin down the ranch dressing with a little buttermilk to use as a creamy and tangy salad dressing.

Drizzle It: Use ranch dressing to add a burst of flavor to grilled chicken, burgers, or sandwiches.

Marinade: Marinate chicken or pork in ranch dressing before grilling or roasting to infuse it with delicious flavors.

Potato Topping: Spoon ranch dressing over baked potatoes or sweet potatoes for a creamy and savory topping.

Veggie Wraps: Spread ranch dressing on tortillas and fill them with fresh vegetables and shredded cheese for a delightful veggie wrap.

With these creative uses, your leftover ranch dressing will never go to waste, and you'll discover new ways to enjoy this beloved dressing beyond fried chicken.

With buttermilk ranch dressing mastered, your fried chicken will have the perfect companion. Whether homemade or store-bought, ranch dressing is a versatile and delightful addition to your culinary repertoire. In the next chapter, we'll explore the world of "Sweet Buttermilk Fried Chicken Desserts," where we'll unveil surprising and delightful, sweet treats featuring fried chicken.

Chapter 9: Buttermilk Fried Chicken and Waffles

In this chapter, we'll explore the ultimate sweet and savory combination – buttermilk fried chicken and waffles. Get ready to indulge in the perfect harmony of crispy fried chicken atop fluffy waffles, and discover classic waffle recipes and creative variations. We'll also help you decide whether to drizzle, use syrup, or combine both for your ideal topping.

9.1 The Ultimate Sweet and Savory Combination

Ingredients:

- Buttermilk fried chicken pieces (from Chapter 2)
- Waffle batter (see recipes in 9.2)

Instructions:

1. Prepare the buttermilk fried chicken as per the classic recipe outlined in Chapter 2, ensuring the chicken is perfectly crispy and flavorful.
2. While the chicken is frying, prepare the waffles according to your chosen recipe or variation (see 9.2).
3. Once the fried chicken and waffles are ready, stack the chicken pieces on top of the waffles to create the ultimate sweet and savory combination.
4. Serve with your favorite toppings or drizzles (see 9.3) and enjoy this delightful fusion of flavors.

9.2 Classic Waffle Recipes and Variations

Here are two classic waffle recipes to get you started, as well as some creative variations:

Classic Belgian Waffles:

Ingredients:

- 2 cups all-purpose flour
- 1 tablespoon granulated sugar
- 1 tablespoon baking powder
- 1/2 teaspoon salt
- 1 3/4 cups buttermilk
- 1/2 cup unsalted butter, melted
- 2 large eggs
- 1 teaspoon vanilla extract

Instructions:

1. In a large mixing bowl, whisk together the flour, sugar, baking powder, and salt.
2. In a separate bowl, whisk together the buttermilk, melted butter, eggs, and vanilla extract.
3. Pour the wet ingredients into the dry ingredients and gently mix until just combined. It's okay if there are a few lumps in the batter.
4. Preheat your waffle iron according to the manufacturer's instructions. Ladle the waffle batter onto the hot waffle iron, spreading it out to the edges. Close the lid and cook until the waffle is golden brown and crispy.
5. Repeat with the remaining batter until all the waffles are cooked.

Classic Buttermilk Waffles:
Ingredients:

- 2 cups all-purpose flour
- 1/4 cup granulated sugar
- 1 tablespoon baking powder
- 1/2 teaspoon baking soda

- 1/2 teaspoon salt
- 1 3/4 cups buttermilk
- 1/2 cup unsalted butter, melted
- 2 large eggs
- 1 teaspoon vanilla extract

Instructions:

1. In a large mixing bowl, whisk together the flour, sugar, baking powder, baking soda, and salt.
2. In a separate bowl, whisk together the buttermilk, melted butter, eggs, and vanilla extract.
3. Pour the wet ingredients into the dry ingredients and gently mix until just combined. Again, it's okay if there are a few lumps in the batter.
4. Preheat your waffle iron and cook the waffles as described in the previous recipe.

Creative Waffle Variations:

1. Chocolate Chip Waffles: Fold in a generous amount of chocolate chips into the waffle batter for a sweet and decadent twist.
2. Blueberry Waffles: Add fresh blueberries to the batter for bursts of sweetness and vibrant color.
3. Cinnamon-Spiced Waffles: Incorporate ground cinnamon and a touch of nutmeg to the batter for a warm and aromatic flavor.
4. Maple Bacon Waffles: Fold crumbled cooked bacon into the waffle batter and drizzle the finished waffles with maple syrup for a delightful savory-sweet combination.
5. Feel free to get creative and experiment with various waffle flavors to find your favorite pairing with the buttermilk fried chicken.

9.3 Drizzle, Syrup, or Both? Finding Your Favorite Topping

When it comes to toppings for buttermilk fried chicken and waffles, there are plenty of delicious options to consider:

Maple Syrup: The classic choice, drizzling warm maple syrup over the crispy fried chicken and fluffy waffles adds a delectable sweetness to the savory dish.

Honey: For a natural and floral sweetness, try drizzling honey over the chicken and waffles.

Hot Sauce: For those who enjoy a bit of heat, a dash of hot sauce adds a zesty kick to the combination.

Spicy Maple Syrup: Combine maple syrup with a pinch of cayenne pepper or hot sauce for a delightful blend of sweet and spicy.

Fruit Compote: Top the chicken and waffles with a homemade fruit compote, such as blueberry or raspberry, for a burst of fruity goodness.

Fried Chicken Gravy: For a truly indulgent treat, pour some rich fried chicken gravy over the waffles and chicken.

Whipped Cream: If you prefer a lighter touch, a dollop of freshly whipped cream adds a touch of creaminess to the dish.

Don't be afraid to mix and match different toppings to find the perfect balance of sweet and savory that suits your taste buds best.

Chapter 10: Gluten-Free Buttermilk Fried Chicken

In this chapter, we'll explore the world of gluten-free buttermilk fried chicken, catering to gluten-free diets without compromising on taste and texture. We'll discuss the best gluten-free flour blends and alternatives to achieve a crispy coating without gluten.

10.1 Catering to Gluten-Free Diets Without Compromising Taste

Ingredients:

- Buttermilk fried chicken pieces (from Chapter 2)
- Gluten-free flour blend for coating (see 10.2)

Instructions:

1. Prepare the buttermilk fried chicken as per the classic recipe outlined in Chapter 2, ensuring the chicken is perfectly brined and seasoned.
2. Once the chicken is ready, coat it with the gluten-free flour blend to achieve a crispy and gluten-free coating.
3. Continue with the frying instructions from Chapter 2.3 to achieve a golden and crispy crust.

10.2 The Best Gluten-Free Flour Blends and Alternatives

When making gluten-free buttermilk fried chicken, you'll need a suitable flour blend for coating. Here are some options:

Gluten-Free All-Purpose Flour Blend: Many stores offer pre-made gluten-free all-purpose flour blends, which are formulated to work as a 1:1 replacement for regular all-purpose flour in recipes.

Rice Flour: Rice flour is naturally gluten-free and provides a light and crispy texture to the coating.

Cornstarch: Cornstarch is another gluten-free alternative that can help achieve a crispy coating.

Chickpea Flour (Gram Flour): Chickpea flour adds a nutty flavor and a crispy texture to the fried chicken.

Almond Flour: For a unique and slightly nutty taste, almond flour can be used as part of the coating mixture.

Potato Starch: Potato starch is a gluten-free option that helps create a crispy crust.

When using gluten-free flour blends or alternatives, ensure they are labeled gluten-free to avoid cross-contamination with gluten-containing ingredients.

10.3 Tips for Achieving a Crispy Coating Without Gluten

Getting a crispy coating without gluten requires a few extra tips and techniques:

Double Dredging: For a thicker and crispier coating, consider double dredging the chicken. After coating the chicken in the gluten-free flour blend, dip it back into the buttermilk and then into the flour again.

Higher Frying Temperature: To ensure a crispy crust, maintain the oil temperature slightly higher than when using regular flour. The hotter oil helps seal the coating quickly, preventing the chicken from becoming greasy.

Drain Excess Buttermilk: Before dredging the chicken in the gluten-free flour blend, shake off any excess buttermilk to prevent the coating from becoming soggy.

Use a Wire Rack: After frying the chicken, place it on a wire rack to allow air circulation and prevent the coating from becoming soggy.

By following these tips and using the right gluten-free flour blend or alternatives, you'll achieve the perfect crispy coating for your gluten-free buttermilk fried chicken.

With gluten-free buttermilk fried chicken mastered, you'll be able to enjoy this delectable dish regardless of dietary restrictions.

Chapter 11: Buttermilk Fried Chicken Salads

In this chapter, we'll explore the delightful fusion of fried chicken and healthy salads. Discover how to incorporate crispy fried chicken into fresh and vibrant salads while maintaining a balance of flavors and textures. We'll also create homemade dressings that complement the dish perfectly.

11.1 Incorporating Fried Chicken into Healthy Salads

Ingredients:

- Buttermilk fried chicken pieces (from Chapter 2)
- Fresh salad greens of your choice (e.g., mixed greens, spinach, arugula)
- Assorted vegetables (e.g., cherry tomatoes, cucumbers, bell peppers)
- Optional toppings (e.g., sliced avocado, shredded cheese, boiled eggs)

Instructions:

1. Prepare the buttermilk fried chicken as per the classic recipe outlined in Chapter 2, ensuring the chicken is crispy and flavorful.
2. While the chicken is frying, wash and prepare the fresh salad greens and vegetables. Chop or slice them as desired.
3. Once the chicken is ready, cut it into bite-sized pieces to top the salads.
4. In a large salad bowl, combine the fresh salad greens, vegetables, and any optional toppings.
5. Add the crispy fried chicken pieces on top of the salad.
6. Drizzle the salad with your preferred homemade dressing (see

11.3) and toss gently to coat the salad evenly.

11.2 Balancing Flavors and Textures

When incorporating fried chicken into salads, it's essential to achieve a harmonious balance of flavors and textures:

Crispy and Juicy: The fried chicken brings a delightful crispy texture and rich flavor to the salad.

Fresh and Crunchy: The salad greens and vegetables provide a fresh and crunchy contrast to the crispy chicken.

Creamy and Tangy: Consider adding creamy and tangy elements, such as avocado, shredded cheese, or a zesty dressing, to balance the richness of the fried chicken.

Sweet and Savory: Incorporate naturally sweet ingredients, like cherry tomatoes or dried fruit, to complement the savory flavors of the chicken.

Nutty and Earthy: Add nuts or seeds for a nutty and earthy note that enhances the overall salad experience.

By thoughtfully combining these elements, you'll create a salad that not only satisfies your taste buds but also provides a delightful range of textures and flavors.

11.3 Homemade Dressings That Complement the Dish

Create homemade dressings to elevate your buttermilk fried chicken salads:

Buttermilk Ranch Dressing (from Chapter 8): The classic buttermilk ranch dressing brings a creamy and herby goodness that pairs wonderfully with the fried chicken.

Honey Mustard Dressing: Mix honey, Dijon mustard, lemon juice, and a touch of olive oil for a sweet and tangy dressing.

Lemon Vinaigrette: Combine fresh lemon juice, olive oil, minced garlic, and a hint of honey for a light and refreshing vinaigrette.

Balsamic Glaze: Drizzle reduced balsamic vinegar over the salad for a rich and sweet-tart flavor.

Creamy Avocado Dressing: Blend ripe avocado, Greek yogurt, lime juice, and cilantro for a creamy and vibrant dressing.

Orange Ginger Dressing: Whisk together orange juice, grated ginger, soy sauce, honey, and sesame oil for a zesty and Asian-inspired dressing.

Experiment with different dressings to find the one that perfectly complements your fried chicken salad.

With buttermilk fried chicken salads mastered, you'll have a delicious and balanced meal that combines the best of both worlds – the indulgence of fried chicken and the freshness of a healthy salad.

Chapter 12: Korean-Style Buttermilk Fried Chicken

In this chapter, we'll embark on a flavorful journey by exploring Korean-style buttermilk fried chicken. We'll discover the unique flavors of Korean fried chicken, including a gochujang glaze and other delightful Korean sauces. Additionally, we'll explore Korean-inspired side dishes to create a complete and satisfying meal.

12.1 Exploring Korean Fried Chicken Flavors

Korean fried chicken is renowned for its crispy texture and bold flavors. Here's how to infuse your buttermilk fried chicken with Korean-inspired tastes:

Ingredients:

- Buttermilk fried chicken pieces (from Chapter 2)

Instructions:

1. Prepare the buttermilk fried chicken as per the classic recipe outlined in Chapter 2, ensuring the chicken is perfectly brined and seasoned.
2. Once the chicken is ready, you'll apply a Korean-style glaze or sauce to add a burst of flavor.

12.2 Gochujang Glaze and Other Korean Sauces
Gochujang Glaze:
Ingredients:

- 1/4 cup gochujang (Korean red pepper paste)
- 2 tablespoons soy sauce
- 2 tablespoons rice vinegar
- 2 tablespoons honey
- 1 tablespoon sesame oil
- 1 teaspoon minced garlic
- 1 teaspoon grated ginger
- 1 tablespoon water (adjust consistency to your liking)

Instructions:

1. In a small saucepan, combine gochujang, soy sauce, rice vinegar, honey, sesame oil, minced garlic, and grated ginger.
2. Cook the mixture over low heat, stirring constantly, until the ingredients are well combined and the glaze is smooth. Add water to adjust the consistency to your desired thickness.
3. Once the glaze is ready, toss the buttermilk fried chicken pieces in the gochujang glaze to coat them with the delicious Korean flavors.

Other Korean Sauces:

Yangnyeom (Korean Sweet and Spicy Sauce): Combine soy sauce, honey, brown sugar, sesame oil, gochugaru (Korean red pepper flakes), minced garlic, and grated ginger for a sweet and spicy sauce.

Garlic Soy Glaze: Mix soy sauce, brown sugar, minced garlic, and a splash of sesame oil for a savory garlic-infused glaze.

Tangy Tamarind Sauce: Blend tamarind paste, honey, soy sauce, rice vinegar, and a pinch of Korean chili powder for a tangy and umami-rich sauce.

12.3 Korean-Inspired Side Dishes

Complete your Korean-style buttermilk fried chicken meal with these delightful Korean-inspired side dishes:

Kimchi Slaw: Toss shredded cabbage and carrots with spicy kimchi, a splash of rice vinegar, and a drizzle of sesame oil for a refreshing and spicy slaw.

Japchae: Stir-fried sweet potato glass noodles with colorful vegetables and a savory sauce made from soy sauce, sesame oil, and sugar.

Korean Radish Pickles: Marinate sliced radishes in a mixture of rice vinegar, sugar, and salt for a tangy and crunchy side dish.

Spinach Namul: Blanch spinach and toss it with sesame oil, soy sauce, minced garlic, and sesame seeds for a simple and flavorful vegetable dish.

With Korean-style buttermilk fried chicken mastered, you'll savor the delightful fusion of crispy fried chicken with bold Korean flavors. Pair it with Korean-inspired side dishes to create a delicious and memorable meal.

Chapter 13: Buttermilk Fried Chicken and Beer Pairing

In this chapter, we'll delve into the art of pairing buttermilk fried chicken with the perfect beer. We'll explore how flavors interact and enhance each other, creating a delightful dining experience. Additionally, we'll provide non-alcoholic beverage alternatives for those who prefer a different type of drink.

13.1 Discovering the Perfect Beer Match for Fried Chicken

Pairing beer with buttermilk fried chicken involves finding a balance of flavors that complement and enhance each other. Here are some beer styles that work well with this classic dish:

Lager: Crisp and refreshing, lagers like Pilsner or American Lager provide a clean palate cleanse, making them an excellent choice to enjoy with fried chicken.

IPA (India Pale Ale): The hoppy bitterness of an IPA contrasts beautifully with the richness of fried chicken, creating a delightful balance of flavors.

Pale Ale: With a balance of malt sweetness and hop bitterness, pale ales are versatile and complement the savory and crispy elements of fried chicken.

Brown Ale: The nutty and caramel notes of a brown ale add depth to the fried chicken experience, creating a comforting and flavorful pairing.

Belgian Witbier: This light and spiced wheat beer provides a refreshing contrast to the fried chicken, making it an interesting and harmonious pairing.

Blonde Ale: Blonde ales have a mild malt profile, making them a smooth and easy-drinking companion to fried chicken.

Remember, beer pairing is subjective, so don't hesitate to experiment with different beer styles to find the one that suits your taste best.

13.2 Understanding How Flavors Interact

When pairing beer with buttermilk fried chicken, consider the following interactions between flavors:

Complementing: Choose a beer that complements the flavors of the fried chicken by enhancing its taste. For example, the hop bitterness in an IPA can cut through the richness of the chicken, making each bite more enjoyable.

Contrasting: Opt for a beer that contrasts the flavors of the fried chicken to create a unique and dynamic experience. For instance, the sweetness of a brown ale can balance the saltiness of the chicken.

Refreshing: Seek a beer with a refreshing quality that cleanses the palate between bites, allowing you to fully appreciate the flavors of both the beer and the fried chicken.

13.3 Non-Alcoholic Beverage Alternatives

For those who prefer non-alcoholic options, there are plenty of delicious alternatives to pair with buttermilk fried chicken:

Sparkling Water: The effervescence of sparkling water provides a refreshing and palate-cleansing experience that complements fried chicken.

Iced Tea: A cold glass of sweetened or unsweetened iced tea offers a classic and satisfying pairing with fried chicken.

Lemonade: Freshly squeezed lemonade brings a tangy and sweet contrast to the savory fried chicken.

Ginger Beer: Non-alcoholic ginger beer provides a zesty and spicy kick that pairs well with the crispy chicken.

Remember to consider personal preferences and flavors when choosing the perfect non-alcoholic beverage to accompany your fried chicken.

With the art of buttermilk fried chicken and beer pairing mastered, you'll elevate your dining experience to new heights.

Chapter 14: Southern Buttermilk Fried Chicken

In this chapter, we'll delve into the world of Southern buttermilk fried chicken, exploring regional variations, traditions, and the cultural significance of this beloved dish. We'll also indulge in classic soul food sides and fixings that perfectly complement the flavors of Southern fried chicken.

14.1 Exploring Regional Variations and Traditions

Southern buttermilk fried chicken is a culinary icon, and its preparation can vary across different regions. Here are some regional variations and traditions:

Nashville Hot Chicken: Originating from Nashville, Tennessee, this variation is known for its fiery spice level. The chicken is coated in a cayenne pepper-infused oil after frying, resulting in a mouthwatering and spicy delight.

Lowcountry Fried Chicken: Hailing from the Lowcountry of South Carolina, this version often features a light buttermilk brine with a touch of hot sauce. The chicken is then dredged in seasoned flour before frying, creating a crispy and flavorful coating.

Kentucky Fried Chicken (KFC): Colonel Harland Sanders popularized his "Kentucky Fried Chicken" recipe, featuring a blend of 11 herbs and spices that became a global sensation.

Georgia Fried Chicken: In Georgia, you might find a sweet tea brine used to infuse the chicken with a subtle hint of sweetness, giving it a unique and refreshing flavor.

Mississippi Fried Chicken: In Mississippi, some families add a hint of paprika or Cajun spices to their buttermilk marinade for a Southern twist on the classic recipe.

14.2 Classic Soul Food Sides and Fixings

Southern buttermilk fried chicken is traditionally served with an array of classic soul food sides and fixings, creating a comforting and satisfying meal. Here are some favorites:

Buttermilk Biscuits: Soft and flaky buttermilk biscuits are a quintessential accompaniment to Southern fried chicken.

Collard Greens: Slow-cooked collard greens seasoned with smoked meat or bacon provide a rich and flavorful side dish.

Macaroni and Cheese: Creamy and cheesy macaroni and cheese is the ultimate comfort food pairing for fried chicken.

Cornbread: Sweet and crumbly cornbread complements the savory flavors of the chicken.

Red Beans and Rice: A hearty and flavorful dish of red beans and rice adds substance to the meal.

Coleslaw: Creamy and tangy coleslaw offers a refreshing contrast to the richness of the fried chicken.

Sweet Potato Casserole: A Southern favorite, sweet potato casserole with marshmallow topping provides a sweet and indulgent side dish.

14.3 The Cultural Significance of Southern Buttermilk Fried Chicken

Southern buttermilk fried chicken holds deep cultural significance in the American South. It is more than just a dish; it represents family gatherings, community celebrations, and cherished traditions. Fried chicken has historical roots in the African American community, where it became a symbol of resourcefulness and creativity in the face of adversity. Its preparation and enjoyment were passed down through generations, becoming a culinary cornerstone of Southern culture.

The dish's popularity spread across the United States and beyond, becoming a symbol of Southern hospitality and comfort food for people of all backgrounds. To this day, Southern buttermilk fried chicken remains an essential part of soul food and Southern cuisine, bringing people together and evoking feelings of warmth and nostalgia.

With the art of Southern buttermilk fried chicken explored, you'll appreciate the regional variations, savor classic soul food sides, and understand the cultural significance of this iconic dish.

Chapter 15: Buttermilk Fried Chicken for Brunch

In this chapter, we'll elevate buttermilk fried chicken to a brunch-worthy status, incorporating eggs and other brunch favorites. We'll explore how to create a delightful brunch experience with fried chicken and suggest cocktail pairings to complete the meal.

15.1 Elevating Fried Chicken to Brunch-Worthy Status

Brunch is the perfect occasion to enjoy a delicious and indulgent meal, and buttermilk fried chicken can shine as a brunch centerpiece. Here's how to make your fried chicken brunch-worthy:

Chicken and Waffles: Combine the crispy fried chicken with fluffy waffles to create a classic and satisfying brunch dish.

Fried Chicken Benedict: Replace the traditional Canadian bacon or ham in Eggs Benedict with fried chicken for a decadent twist.

Breakfast Sandwich: Assemble a mouthwatering breakfast sandwich with fried chicken, a runny fried egg, cheese, and your favorite condiments between a biscuit or a buttery croissant.

Chicken and Biscuits: Serve fried chicken alongside freshly baked biscuits, offering a delectable combination of savory and flaky goodness.

Chicken and Avocado Toast: Top avocado toast with a piece of fried chicken for a brunch dish that's both trendy and delicious.

15.2 Incorporating Eggs and Brunch Favorites

Incorporate eggs and other brunch favorites into your buttermilk fried chicken dishes:

Chicken and Waffles with Sunny-Side-Up Eggs:
Ingredients:

- Buttermilk fried chicken pieces (from Chapter 2)
- Waffle batter (from Chapter 9.2)
- Eggs
- Maple syrup

Instructions:

1. Prepare the buttermilk fried chicken as per the classic recipe outlined in Chapter 2.
2. While the chicken is frying, prepare the waffles according to the recipe in Chapter 9.2.
3. In a separate skillet, fry the eggs sunny-side-up, keeping the yolk runny.
4. Once the fried chicken and waffles are ready, stack the chicken pieces on top of the waffles, and place a sunny-side-up egg on each chicken piece.
5. Drizzle with maple syrup and enjoy the delicious combination of crispy fried chicken, fluffy waffles, and perfectly cooked eggs.

Fried Chicken Benedict:
Ingredients:

- Buttermilk fried chicken pieces (from Chapter 2)
- English muffins, halved and toasted
- Poached eggs (see poaching instructions below)
- Hollandaise sauce (store-bought or homemade)

Instructions:

1. Prepare the buttermilk fried chicken as per the classic recipe outlined in Chapter 2.
2. While the chicken is frying, toast the English muffins and prepare the poached eggs.

Poaching Eggs:

1. Fill a large saucepan with water and bring it to a gentle simmer.
2. Add a splash of vinegar to the water (optional; it helps the egg

whites coagulate more quickly).

3. Carefully crack each egg into a small bowl, one at a time.

4. Create a gentle whirlpool in the simmering water by stirring it with a spoon.

5. Gently slide the cracked egg into the center of the whirlpool, allowing the swirling water to envelop the egg white around the yolk.

6. Cook the egg for about 3-4 minutes for a runny yolk or longer for a firmer yolk.

7. Use a slotted spoon to remove the poached egg from the water, draining any excess water, and place it on a plate lined with a paper towel.

8. Once the fried chicken and English muffins are ready, assemble the Fried Chicken Benedict by placing a piece of fried chicken on each toasted English muffin half.

9. Top each chicken with a poached egg and generously drizzle hollandaise sauce over the eggs.

10. Serve immediately and enjoy this luxurious and brunch-worthy variation of Eggs Benedict.

15.3 Brunch Cocktail Pairings

Complete your buttermilk fried chicken brunch with these delightful cocktail pairings:

Mimosa: The classic brunch cocktail of champagne and orange juice adds a sparkling and refreshing touch to your meal.

Bloody Mary: A savory and spicy Bloody Mary provides a bold and flavorful pairing with fried chicken.

Michelada: This Mexican beer cocktail with lime juice, hot sauce, and spices complements the savory and zesty flavors of fried chicken.

Bellini: A Bellini made with peach puree and prosecco offers a sweet and fruity contrast to the crispy chicken.

Southern Iced Tea Cocktail: Mix sweet tea, bourbon, and a splash of lemon juice for a Southern-inspired beverage that pairs well with fried chicken.

With buttermilk fried chicken elevated to a brunch-worthy delight, you'll have a truly memorable meal that's perfect for leisurely weekend mornings. Whether you prefer chicken and waffles, a Fried Chicken Benedict, or any other brunch variation, you'll create a comforting and indulgent experience that will make your brunch guests rave.

Chapter 16: Buttermilk Fried Chicken Stir-Fry

In this chapter, we'll give buttermilk fried chicken an Asian-inspired twist by incorporating it into a flavorful stir-fry. We'll explore how to create a balanced stir-fry with vegetables and sauces, and suggest pairing options with rice, noodles, or greens.

16.1 Giving Fried Chicken an Asian-Inspired Twist

By incorporating buttermilk fried chicken into an Asian-inspired stir-fry, we can infuse the dish with delicious flavors and textures. Here's how to create a mouthwatering Asian-inspired stir-fry with fried chicken:

Cut the Fried Chicken: Cut the fried chicken into bite-sized pieces to make it easy to incorporate into the stir-fry and ensure even distribution of flavors.

Stir-Fry Sauce: Prepare a savory and umami-rich stir-fry sauce using ingredients like soy sauce, oyster sauce, hoisin sauce, garlic, ginger, and a touch of sweetness from honey or brown sugar.

Fresh Vegetables: Add a variety of fresh vegetables like bell peppers, broccoli, snap peas, carrots, and scallions to the stir-fry for color, crunch, and nutrition.

Aromatic Ingredients: Include aromatic ingredients like garlic, ginger, and green onions to enhance the overall flavor profile of the stir-fry.

16.2 Creating a Balanced Stir-Fry with Veggies and Sauces
Ingredients:

- Buttermilk fried chicken pieces (from Chapter 2), cut into bite-sized pieces
- Assorted fresh vegetables (bell peppers, broccoli, snap peas,

carrots, etc.), sliced or chopped
- Aromatic ingredients (garlic, ginger, green onions), minced
- Stir-fry sauce (see recipe below)
- Cooking oil (vegetable or peanut oil)
- Sesame seeds (optional, for garnish)

Stir-Fry Sauce:
Ingredients:

- 1/4 cup soy sauce
- 2 tablespoons oyster sauce
- 1 tablespoon hoisin sauce
- 1 tablespoon rice vinegar
- 1 tablespoon honey or brown sugar
- 1 teaspoon sesame oil
- 1/2 cup chicken or vegetable broth

Instructions:

1. In a small bowl, whisk together all the ingredients for the stir-fry sauce. Set aside.
2. In a wok or large skillet, heat cooking oil over medium-high heat.
3. Add the minced garlic, ginger, and green onions to the hot oil and stir-fry for about 30 seconds or until fragrant.
4. Add the assorted vegetables to the wok and stir-fry for 2-3 minutes until they begin to soften but are still crisp.
5. Push the vegetables to one side of the wok and add the bite-sized pieces of buttermilk fried chicken to the other side.
6. Pour the stir-fry sauce over the chicken and vegetables. Toss everything together to coat evenly and cook for an additional 2-3 minutes until the chicken is heated through and the sauce thickens slightly.
7. Remove the wok from the heat and garnish the stir-fry with sesame seeds, if desired.

16.3 Pairing with Rice, Noodles, or Greens

To complete the buttermilk fried chicken stir-fry, you can serve it with your choice of accompaniments:

Steamed Jasmine Rice: The fragrant and fluffy Jasmine rice complements the savory stir-fry, soaking up the delicious sauce.

Stir-Fried Noodles: Choose your favorite noodles (e.g., rice noodles, chow mein, udon) and stir-fry them separately or toss them with the chicken and vegetables for a noodle stir-fry.

Cauliflower Rice: For a low-carb option, serve the stir-fry with cauliflower rice, a healthier alternative to traditional rice.

Leafy Greens: Opt for a bed of fresh greens, such as baby spinach or arugula, to serve the stir-fry on top of for a lighter and vibrant option.

With buttermilk fried chicken given an Asian-inspired twist in a flavorful stir-fry, you'll enjoy the best of both worlds – the indulgence of fried chicken and the bold flavors of Asian cuisine. Whether you pair it with rice, noodles, or greens, this dish will become a satisfying and unforgettable addition to your culinary repertoire.

Chapter 17: Buttermilk Fried Chicken Sliders

In this chapter, we'll explore the world of buttermilk fried chicken sliders – perfect for parties and gatherings. We'll learn how to create mini-sized, flavorful sandwiches that are sure to be a hit with guests. Additionally, we'll dive into slider-themed party ideas to make your event a memorable one.

17.1 Perfect for Parties and Gatherings

Buttermilk fried chicken sliders are a fantastic choice for parties and gatherings for several reasons:

Miniature Delights: Sliders are cute and bite-sized, making them easy to handle and perfect for sampling different flavors.

Crowd-Pleasers: Who can resist a flavorful buttermilk fried chicken sandwich? Sliders are sure to please guests of all ages.

Versatility: Sliders can be customized with various toppings and sauces, catering to different tastes and dietary preferences.

Easy to Serve: Sliders are convenient to serve, allowing guests to grab and enjoy them at their leisure.

17.2 Creating Mini-Sized, Flavorful Sandwiches
Ingredients:

- Buttermilk fried chicken pieces (from Chapter 2), cut into smaller portions to fit the slider buns
- Slider buns or mini burger buns
- Lettuce leaves
- Sliced tomatoes
- Pickles
- Your choice of condiments and sauces (mayonnaise, mustard, ketchup, barbecue sauce, etc.)

Instructions:

1. Prepare the buttermilk fried chicken as per the classic recipe outlined in Chapter 2, cutting the chicken into smaller portions to fit the slider buns.
2. Slice the slider buns in half horizontally and lightly toast them if desired.
3. Assemble the sliders by placing a piece of fried chicken on the bottom half of each slider bun.
4. Add a lettuce leaf, sliced tomatoes, and pickles on top of the chicken.
5. Spread your choice of condiments and sauces on the top half of the slider bun and place it on top to complete the mini sandwich.
6. Secure the sliders with toothpicks to keep them together during serving.

17.3 Slider-Themed Party Ideas

To make your buttermilk fried chicken slider party a hit, consider these slider-themed party ideas:

Slider Bar: Set up a slider bar with various toppings, sauces, and condiments, allowing guests to customize their sliders to their liking. Offer a variety of cheeses, bacon, avocado, caramelized onions, coleslaw, and more.

Slider Trio Platters: Create platters with different slider variations, showcasing various flavor combinations. Offer classic sliders with traditional toppings, spicy sliders with hot sauces and jalapenos, and gourmet sliders with unique ingredients.

Slider Pairings: Pair different types of sliders with specific beers, wines, or cocktails. Provide tasting notes and recommendations to guide guests in their pairings.

Slider Showdown: Host a friendly slider competition, where guests can submit their own slider creations and vote for their favorites. Offer small prizes or gift cards to the winners.

Slider Buffet: Set up a buffet with a variety of sliders, side dishes, and desserts. Encourage guests to try different combinations and enjoy a slider feast.

With buttermilk fried chicken sliders, you'll have a party food that's both fun and delicious. Whether you're hosting a casual get-together or a festive celebration, these mini-sized sandwiches will be a hit with everyone.

Chapter 18: Buttermilk Fried Chicken Poutine

In this chapter, we'll explore the fusion of buttermilk fried chicken and poutine, creating a delightful twist on this classic Canadian dish. We'll learn how to make the best poutine gravy to complement the fried chicken and explore creative poutine variations to elevate the dish to new heights.

18.1 A Fusion Dish with a Delightful Twist

Poutine is a beloved Canadian comfort food traditionally made with French fries, cheese curds, and savory gravy. By adding crispy and flavorful buttermilk fried chicken to the mix, we create a delicious fusion dish that brings together the best of both worlds.

18.2 Making the Best Poutine Gravy

Ingredients:

- 2 tablespoons unsalted butter
- 2 tablespoons all-purpose flour
- 2 cups beef or chicken broth
- 1 cup beef or chicken drippings (from cooking the fried chicken)
- Salt and pepper to taste

Instructions:

1. In a saucepan, melt the butter over medium heat.
2. Add the flour to the melted butter, whisking constantly to form a smooth roux. Cook the roux for a few minutes until it turns a golden brown color.
3. Slowly pour in the broth, whisking continuously to prevent lumps from forming.
4. Add the beef or chicken drippings to the saucepan, stirring well

to combine.

5. Bring the mixture to a simmer and cook for a few minutes until the gravy thickens to your desired consistency.

6. Season the gravy with salt and pepper to taste.

The rich and savory poutine gravy will add a delightful layer of flavor to the buttermilk fried chicken and cheese curds.

18.3 Exploring Creative Poutine Variations

While the classic buttermilk fried chicken poutine is delicious on its own, you can also explore creative variations to add unique twists to the dish:

Spicy Buffalo Chicken Poutine: Toss the fried chicken in Buffalo sauce before assembling the poutine for a spicy and tangy kick.

Southern BBQ Chicken Poutine: Drizzle the fried chicken with your favorite BBQ sauce, adding a Southern flair to the dish.

Kimchi Fried Chicken Poutine: Incorporate Korean-inspired flavors by topping the poutine with kimchi and a drizzle of gochujang sauce.

Maple Bacon Chicken Poutine: Add maple-glazed bacon to the poutine, creating a sweet and savory combination that's hard to resist.

Mediterranean Chicken Poutine: Top the poutine with sliced olives, roasted red peppers, feta cheese, and a sprinkle of oregano for a Mediterranean twist.

Tex-Mex Chicken Poutine: Combine Mexican and American flavors by adding guacamole, jalapenos, and a dollop of sour cream to the poutine.

Get creative with your toppings and experiment with different flavors to create your own unique buttermilk fried chicken poutine variations.

With buttermilk fried chicken poutine, you'll experience the delectable combination of crispy chicken, cheese curds, and savory gravy, creating a comforting and indulgent meal. Whether you enjoy the classic version or explore creative variations, this fusion dish will surely become a favorite on your menu.

Chapter 19: Air Fryer Buttermilk Fried Chicken

In this chapter, we'll explore the world of air fryer buttermilk fried chicken, a delicious alternative that allows you to enjoy the crispy goodness of fried chicken with fewer calories. We'll provide tips for achieving crispy results in an air fryer and compare air frying to traditional frying.

19.1 Enjoying Fried Chicken with Fewer Calories

Air frying offers a healthier alternative to traditional deep-frying by using hot air to cook the food instead of submerging it in oil. With an air fryer, you can achieve a crispy and golden exterior while significantly reducing the amount of oil used, resulting in a fried chicken that's lighter on calories but still packed with flavor.

19.2 Tips for Achieving Crispy Results in an Air Fryer

To ensure your buttermilk fried chicken turns out crispy and delicious in the air fryer, follow these tips:

Preheat the Air Fryer: Always preheat your air fryer before adding the chicken. Preheating ensures that the hot air circulates evenly, resulting in a crispy exterior.

Use Cooking Spray: Lightly coat the chicken with cooking spray or brush it with a small amount of oil. This will help promote browning and crispiness.

Don't Overcrowd: Avoid overcrowding the air fryer basket. Arrange the chicken in a single layer with some space between each piece to allow the hot air to circulate properly.

Flip or Shake: Halfway through the cooking time, flip the chicken pieces or give the basket a gentle shake to ensure even cooking and browning on all sides.

Monitor Cooking Time: Keep a close eye on the chicken as it cooks in the air fryer. Cooking times can vary depending on the size of the chicken pieces and the air fryer model.

Use a Meat Thermometer: For larger pieces of chicken, such as thighs or breasts, use a meat thermometer to ensure the chicken reaches a safe internal temperature of 165°F (74°C).

19.3 Air Frying vs. Traditional Frying: A Comparison
Air Frying:

- Requires little to no oil, making it a healthier option with fewer calories and less fat.
- Produces a crispy exterior with a tender and juicy interior.
- Reduces the risk of splattering hot oil, making it safer to use.
- Requires preheating the air fryer for best results.
- May take slightly longer to cook compared to traditional frying.

Traditional Frying:

Uses a significant amount of oil for deep frying, resulting in a higher calorie and fat content.

- Creates a crispy exterior and juicy interior but can sometimes lead to a greasier end product.
- Carries a higher risk of hot oil splatters, making it more hazardous.
- Requires less cooking time due to the higher oil temperature.
- Requires careful temperature control to avoid burning the chicken or uneven cooking.

Both air frying and traditional frying have their pros and cons, but air frying provides a healthier option without compromising on taste and texture.

With air fryer buttermilk fried chicken, you can indulge in the crispy goodness of fried chicken with fewer calories and less oil. By following the tips for achieving crispy results and understanding the differences between air frying and traditional frying, you'll master the art of air fryer fried chicken.

Chapter 20: Buttermilk Fried Chicken Desserts

In thisfinal chapter, we'll explore the world of buttermilk fried chicken desserts – surprising sweet treats that feature the delicious flavors of fried chicken. We'll venture into dessert waffles, donuts, and more, discovering unconventional yet delicious flavor combinations that will excite your taste buds.

20.1 Surprising Sweet Treats Featuring Fried Chicken

Who said fried chicken is just for savory dishes? By incorporating it into desserts, we create a delightful surprise that combines sweet and savory flavors in a unique and delicious way. Get ready to indulge in the unexpected!

20.2 Dessert Waffles, Donuts, and More

Chicken and Waffle Ice Cream Sandwiches:

Create a fun and unique ice cream sandwich by sandwiching a scoop of your favorite ice cream between two mini buttermilk waffles and a small piece of buttermilk fried chicken.

Fried Chicken Donuts:

Combine the flavors of fried chicken and donuts by topping a freshly glazed donut with a small piece of crispy fried chicken. The sweet and savory combination is truly indulgent.

Chicken and Pancake Skewers:

Thread small pieces of buttermilk fried chicken and mini pancake bites onto skewers. Serve them with maple syrup for dipping, creating a playful and tasty treat.

Fried Chicken Beignets:

Mix up a beignet batter and fold in small pieces of buttermilk fried chicken. Fry the beignets until golden brown, and dust them with powdered sugar for a delightful sweet and savory pastry.

Maple Butter Chicken Biscuits:

Spread warm biscuits with a sweet and creamy maple butter, and top them with small pieces of buttermilk fried chicken. The combination of buttery biscuits, maple sweetness, and savory chicken is divine.

20.3 Unconventional Yet Delicious Flavor Combinations

As you venture into the realm of buttermilk fried chicken desserts, consider these unconventional flavor combinations that surprisingly work together:

Sweet and Spicy: Add a drizzle of honey or a sprinkle of cinnamon sugar to your fried chicken for a sweet and spicy contrast.

Chocolate and Chicken: Dip small pieces of buttermilk fried chicken in melted chocolate for a decadent and unexpected treat.

Fruit Infusion: Pair fried chicken with fruity flavors by adding a dollop of fruit preserves or a side of fruit compote.

Citrus Zest: Sprinkle some citrus zest, such as orange or lemon, on your fried chicken to add a bright and refreshing note.

Nutty Crunch: Crush some candied nuts and sprinkle them over the fried chicken for an additional layer of texture and flavor.

With buttermilk fried chicken desserts, you'll embark on a culinary adventure that combines sweet and savory in surprising and delightful ways. From ice cream sandwiches to fried chicken beignets, these treats will be a unique and memorable addition to your dessert repertoire.

Congratulations! You've completed the cookbook, "Buttermilk Fried Chicken: A Flavorful Journey." With its extensive collection of recipes and creative twists, this cookbook will inspire both novice and experienced chefs to explore the diverse and delicious world of buttermilk fried chicken. Whether you're hosting a family dinner, a brunch party, or a global-inspired feast, the recipes in this cookbook will be sure to impress and satisfy your guests.

Happy cooking and enjoy your flavorful journey with buttermilk fried chicken!

In this cookbook, "Buttermilk Fried Chicken: A Flavorful Journey," we embarked on a culinary adventure exploring the diverse and delicious world of buttermilk fried chicken. From classic recipes to international twists and surprising dessert treats, we discovered the versatility and indulgence that this beloved dish has to offer.

We began by mastering the art of the classic buttermilk fried chicken, learning the importance of a flavorful brine, the perfect blend of spices, and achieving a crispy golden crust. From there, we explored a range of variations and accompaniments, from spicy and Korean-inspired to healthier oven-baked options and even integrating fried chicken into salads and sandwiches.

We took buttermilk fried chicken beyond the traditional savory realm, creating brunch-worthy dishes with eggs and exploring its fusion with poutine and international cuisines. From Southern soul food to Asian-inspired stir-fries, our fried chicken journey spanned the globe, offering unique flavors and culinary experiences.

We didn't stop at savory delights – we dared to venture into dessert territory, discovering the surprising and delightful combinations of fried chicken in ice cream sandwiches, donuts, and more. Unconventional yet delicious flavor pairings left our taste buds tingling with excitement.

Throughout this culinary journey, we learned valuable tips and techniques for achieving crispy results, elevating the dish to new heights. Whether air frying for a healthier option or creating a slider bar for a fun party theme, we discovered the endless possibilities of buttermilk fried chicken.

This cookbook is a celebration of the joy and satisfaction that comes from cooking and enjoying a beloved comfort food with a touch of creativity and innovation. From family gatherings to festive occasions, buttermilk fried chicken is a dish that brings people together, creating cherished memories and satisfying appetites.

As you continue your culinary adventures, remember the art and craft of buttermilk fried chicken – the blend of flavors, the balance of textures, and the joy of sharing a delicious meal with loved ones. May this cookbook inspire you to explore, experiment, and savor the delightful world of buttermilk fried chicken.

Happy cooking and bon appétit!